*re·cy·cle:*   *verb*   \(ˌ)rē-ˈsī-kəl\
*: to make something new from (something that has been used before)*
*: to send (used newspapers, bottles, cans, etc.) to a place where*
  *they are made into something new*
*: to use (something) again*

*Synonyms: reuse, reclaim, recover.*

Merriam-Webster Dictionary

L.T. always recycles.

Uses discarded and unwanted things to create
new and useful inventions.

L.T. is described as imaginative, resourceful and
very creative.  He redesigns and transforms just
about everything he gets his hands on, making
something old – New Again!

L.T. believes in reducing waste, reusing things,
going green  and recycling for life
to Save Our Planet.

My everlasting gratitude to:
All the dedicated and wonderful
people who recycle, go green,
protect the environment and
help save our planet for future
generations.

My young readers, who are the
hopes for a better future and a
greener world for others to enjoy.

My beloved, "my chicks"
Beano, Nancy, Liz, Pat, Sue
& Trude and my friends for their
support and encouragement.

–Tom Noll ♻

To Caitlyn, Evan and Blake.

–Brandon Fall ♻

To Hinako, Machi, Yu,
Honoka & Shiho.

–Kimiyo Nishio ♻

Printed on 100% Recycled paper and
with eco-friendly soy ink!

"Trash to Treasure" Series - Recycling Creatively with L.T. – "Selling Eggs"
Written by: Tom Noll
Illustrated by: Brandon Fall & Kimiyo Nishio
Edited by: Alberto Ucles
Copyright © 2015 by Green Kids Press
Printed in Hong Kong

ISBN - 13: 978-1-939377-58-6 Hardcover
ISBN - 10: 1939377587
Library of Congress Control Number: 2014952863
UPC -   850924005021
First Edition

For information about custom editions, special sales, premium and
corporate purchases, please email us at: Alberto@greenkidspress.com

Signature Book Printing, Inc.
www.sbpbooks.com

**Green Kids Press, LLC™**
Nurturing Imagination & Creativity
GreenKidsPress.com

23 T Street NW – Washington, DC 20001-1008
SAN-920-458X
(202) 518-7070
Fax (202) 588-0931
Alberto@greenkidspress.com
www.GreenKidsPress.com
www.LTsRecyclingWorld.com

# Selling Eggs

Written by Tom Noll
Illustrated by Brandon Fall &
Kimiyo Nishio

*Keep Recycling*

*Tom Noll*

In the small town of Greenville, not very far away, lives a young boy named L.T. who is known for his creative recycling ideas. He has a recycled bike, a recycled fence in his yard and even two recycled pets - a dog named Rex and a cat named Sebastian that he rescued from the animal shelter. L.T.'s dad, also has a recycled rainbow truck.

"One man's trash is my treasure!" L.T. likes to say.

Whenever L.T. visits his grandparents' farm,
he puts his favorite chicken Sara, on the handlebars
of his recycled bike and gives her a ride around the
barnyard. Sara ruffles her feathers and squawks
with excitement, and always lays an egg.

One summer, L.T.'s grandparents wanted to go on vacation. They asked L.T. to take care of the chickens while they were away. L.T. loved collecting the eggs that Sara and the other chickens laid in their nesting boxes every day.

When his grandparents came back, L.T. asked his Dad if he could have some chickens of his own.

"Okay, L.T., as you did a good job taking care of Grandma's chickens" Dad answered. "You can order twelve chickens from Grandma's poultry catalog."

L.T. told Sue; "Twelve chickens will give me one dozen eggs a day!" L.T. exclaimed. "That's a lot of eggs! I can sell them for pocket money!"

L.T. sees a section in the catalog that says "Game Birds" and asks Grandma: "What kind of games do they play?"

Grandma smiles and said, "Oh L.T., that's another name for quail, pheasants and wild turkeys." They both laugh and with Grandma's help, L.T. filled out the order form and mailed it off. Then he waited...waited and waited.

Finally, the mailman brought a "Special Delivery" package with holes in it. When L.T. opened the box, he saw twelve fuzzy colorful chicks inside. They were chirping loudly.

"I ordered chickens!" L.T. exclaimed. "Why did they send me chicks? Chicks can't lay eggs!"

"Chicks grow fast, L.T." Dad said. "You'll see. But we need to get a light bulb to keep them warm, so it will be like being under their mother's wings." L.T. and his dad hung a light bulb over the box and plugged it in. It was warm, but not all the chicks fit under the light at one time, and they were still chirping loudly.

L.T. went to the attic to see what else he could find that might help keep the chicks warm. He found a large green lampshade. Then he remembered that his sister Sue had a long feather boa. That would be just like the chicks' mother's wings! L.T. put the lampshade over the bulb and wrapped the boa around the bottom. The chicks ran under the warm lamp and settled down happily.

Sue was so impressed with the fun lamp that she asked if she could have it for her bedroom. Since the chicks grew up so fast, she gave L.T. her big dollhouse so the chicks would have more room.

Once L.T. fixed the dollhouse with straw, the chicks ran in and got comfy.

The chicks got bigger every day, and L.T. realized that they would soon need a bigger place to live. So L.T. and his dad went to their favorite place, Mr. Savage's "Recycleville" junkyard and recycling center, where L.T. found two birdcages.

"These are perfect!" he said, holding them up high. "Chicks are birds, and birds need a cage!"

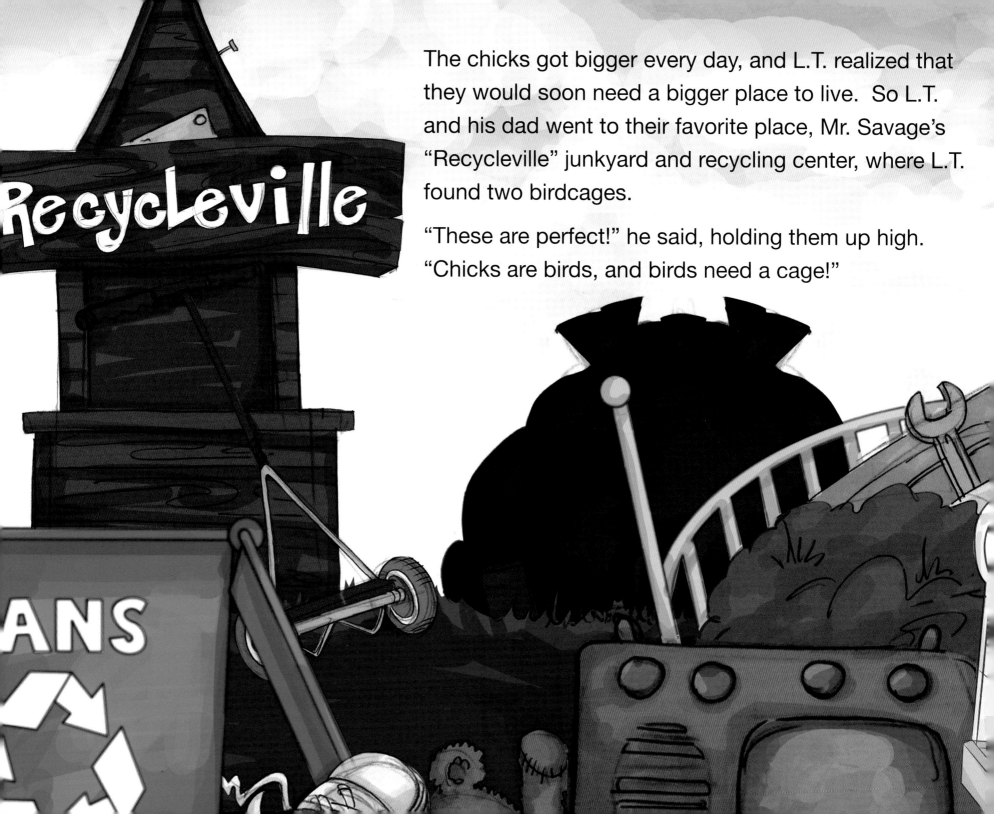

When they got home, L.T. put six chicks in each recycled birdcage. Then he placed one birdcage on each handle bar of his bicycle and went into town to show everyone his chicks.

"Soon I'll be collecting one dozen eggs a day!" he bragged.

As the chicks grew bigger, L.T. had to get another birdcage, and then another. When they no longer fit in the birdcages, L.T. taught the chicks to ride on his handlebars, just like Sara.

ecycle Shop

Our family recycles

Finally the chicks were full grown and ready to start laying eggs. "It's time to get them a nesting box," said L.T.'s dad.

As usual, L.T. had another creative recycling idea! He found an old wooden fruit crate and filled it with recycled Easter basket grass. Then he attached the crate to the back of his bike.

9

L.T. asked his mom for paint and a brush.

"What are you painting, L.T.?" asked Mom.

L.T. grinned. "You know how Grandma and Grandpa sell 'farm fresh eggs'?"

Mom nodded.

"Well, I'm going to sell 'bicycle fresh eggs'!" said L.T.

As L.T. rides his bike thru town the chickens take turns sitting in the box and laying their eggs. Now L.T. is selling his 'bicycle fresh eggs' to everyone.

As he sells his eggs, he wonders what his next creative recycling adventure will be!

The all-grown-up L.T. has his own 1950's recycled rainbow truck, bicycle and white bicycle fence. Do you think he still sells "Bicycle Fresh Eggs"?

# Bicycle Fences

Original Manassas, VA by Tom Noll

Washington, DC: Bloomingdale (Rhode Island Ave & 1st St NW) by Tom Noll

WDC-Easter

WDC-Halloween

WDC-Christmas

Upper Marlboro, MD

Somerset, OH by Tom Noll

Alexandria, VA by Heather & Rob

# To Our Young Readers:

Join L.T.'s Recycling Club and take his "Recycling, Going Green & Saving the Planet Pledge" to earn your Recycling Certificate. Share the information below with your parents, grandparents, brothers, sisters, relatives, friends, teachers, and classmates. All of Us Together, doing just a couple of the things listed below, can make a big difference in Protecting Our Planet!

**Things We All Can Do To Take Care and Save Our Planet Earth For Future Generations:**

1. *WE can* sort and recycle trash properly in the designated bins or containers for: paper, plastic, glass, and aluminum. This way it can be reused to create new products and toys for us to enjoy.

2. *WE can* keep our homes, gardens, sidewalks, streets, schools, playgrounds, and parks clean. We can put trash in appropriate trashcans or recycle bins, and not litter our planet.

3. *WE can* plant trees, bushes, and flowers. They make the world prettier, help clean the air that we breathe, provide shade in the summer, and protect us in the winter.

4. *WE can* choose to walk, ride a bike, or use public transportation (buses, subways, trains) with an adult, instead of driving a car. We can share rides for longer trips with our family or friends. Cars create pollution, which harms the environment.

5. *WE can* turn off lights and electronic equipment (TV, computer, stereo, air conditioner) when not in use or when we leave a room. We can also unplug chargers when not charging an appliance. It will save energy and money.

6. *WE can* keep our thermostat at a reasonable temperature, and, if we get chilly, we can put on a sweater. Let's make sure our parents insulate the home and seal cracks around windows and doors; it will keep the heat inside the home.

7. *WE can* keep doors and windows closed so we do not waste air conditioning in the summer or heat in the winter. It will save energy and money.

8. **WE can** replace old light bulbs with energy-saving, compact fluorescent bulbs. We can also look for the energy efficient symbol on new appliances. It will save a lot of energy and money.

9. **WE can** conserve water. We can take shorter showers and baths. When brushing our teeth, or when our dad is shaving, or our mom is washing something in the kitchen, only run the water when you need to use it. Report and fix water leaks, so we do not waste water.

10. **WE can** reduce the amount of paper we use at home and school. We can use paper on both sides, when we write or draw. We can also reuse old paper for class lessons or projects and then recycle it when we are done. We can buy recycled paper. We can save many trees this way.

11. **WE can** use reusable and recycled bags when we go shopping. We can buy recycled products and environmentally friendly cleaners and other items.

12. **WE can** find other uses for things we no longer need. We can put on our inventor caps and find creative ways to reuse and enjoy them.

13. **WE can** donate clothes, books, toys, or things we and our family can't use anymore to churches, charity organizations, or second hand stores, so others can enjoy them.

14. **WE can** enjoy the freshest and healthiest food by creating our own small garden at home or in a community garden. We can buy local and natural products when possible. We can support our local farmer's markets and businesses.

15. **WE can** get a recycled pet. We can adopt our dog, cat, or favorite pet from a rescue center or animal shelter. They will love us unconditionally forever and a day!

Reduce. Reuse. Recycle
CREATIVELY SAVING OUR PLANET
LTsRecyclingWorld.com

# "Recycling, Going Green & Saving the Planet Pledge"

**I Pledge To Take Care of Mother Earth For Future Generations by:**

- Reducing waste by sorting and recycling trash properly in the designated bins.
- Reusing things by finding creative ways to restore and recreate them.
- Choosing to walk, ride a bike or use public transportation when possible, to avoid pollution.
- Saving energy by turning off lights and appliances when not in use.
- Planting trees, bushes, and flowers for a greener and ecofriendly environment.
- Conserving water by taking shorter showers and baths, or when brushing my teeth.
- Using reusable and recycled bags when shopping.
- Adopting my pet, from a rescue center or animal shelter when possible.

LT
Recycling
Hero

## Tom Noll, Author

Tom is an artist, sculptor, landscape designer, avid nature lover, recycler and advocate for going green. Tom is a native of Somerset, Ohio and is a first-time writer who lives in the Washington, D.C. metropolitan area. He won the Gold Mom's Choice Award® for his first book "The Bicycle Fence. For the 15 years that he lived in Manassas, VA, he was known for his imaginative white bicycle fence at his home, which he decorated for major holidays.
**www.LTsRecyclingWorld.com**

## Brandon Fall, Illustrator

Brandon has always loved illustration and spent countless hours of his childhood getting lost in his drawings. He is now fortunate to make a living continuing to do what he loves from his home in California. Brandon's illustration and design work has appeared in a number of publications and has won awards. When he's not illustrating, he enjoys spending time with his wife and children in the beautiful outdoors.
**www.fallillustration.com**

## Kimiyo Nishio, Illustrator

Kimiyo is a graphic designer and illustrator based in sunny greater Los Angeles area, California. Kimiyo loves print design such as creating logos and packaging, but illustration has been her all time favorite thing to do since she was a little girl. Regardless of what she creates, she is passionate about what she does and loves to inspire people by creating something that speaks to their heart.
**kimiyonishio.squarespace.com**

## Visit www.LTsRecyclingWorld.com

For the latest information on L.T. and his adventures in creative recycling join L.T.'s Recycling Club and take his "Recycling, Going Green & Saving the Planet Pledge." You can also download it, activity sheets, Q & As, coloring pages and games about recycling.

Send us photos of your recycling ideas, projects or bicycle fences that you create with your family, friends, or teachers, at school or in your community. We will feature them on L.T.'s website for all to learn from, admire and enjoy.

### Green Kids Press, LLC™
Nurturing Imagination & Creativity
GreenKidsPress.com

## Remember to Celebrate Every Year:
## Earth Day, April 22 and America Recycles Day, Nov 15th

L.T. recommends the following books about recycling & going green that he enjoyed:

"Why Should I?"- Series: Recycle, Protect Nature, Save Energy and Save Water.

"Disney- Mickey Go Green: A Family Guide to a Sustainable Lifestyle"

"Abby's Adventures: Earth Day and the Recycling Fashionista"

"Michael Recycles Series"

"The Everything Green Classroom Book"

"Earth Book for Kids"

"What Does it Mean to be Green"

"The Adventures of a Plastic Bottle"

# L.T.'s Recycling Facts

## Together We Can Make a Difference in Protecting and Saving Our Planet Today!

Recycling is a continuous effort made by all of us, and an endless loop that only works best if the collected materials are transformed into new products that can be reused or sold, bought and used again. Many things we normally throw away can be recycled; including paper, plastic, glass, aluminum, steel and so many other things we use in our daily life. Recycling conserves and protects our precious natural resources such as trees, water and minerals. The results of going green are clear: recycling provides cleaner air, water and land, less pollution, more forested land and open spaces, reduced greenhouse gases and a healthier environment. Recycling also saves money!

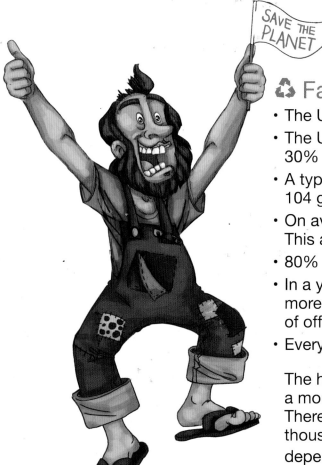

## Let's remember L.T.'s 3 R's:
## Reduce Waste, Reuse Things and Recycle Always!

### Facts

- The United States (US) is the #1 trash-producing country in the world.
- The US represents only 5% of the world's population, but it generates 30% of the world's waste.
- A typical American family consumes 182 gallons of soda, 29 gallons of juice, 104 gallons of milk and 26 gallons of bottled water a year.
- On average, each one of us produces 4.4 pounds of solid waste each day. This adds up to almost a ton of trash per person, per year.
- 80% of US products are used once and then thrown away.
- In a year Americans will throw away over 1million tons of aluminum cans and foil, more than 11 million tons of glass bottles and jars, over 4 and a half million tons of office paper, and nearly 10 million tons of newspaper.
- Every day, Americans create 251 million tons of trash that ends up in landfills and incinerators.

The highest point in Hamilton County, Ohio (near Cincinnati) is "Mount Rumpke." It is actually a mountain of trash at the Rumpke sanitary landfill towering 1,045 ft. above sea level. There are 3,091 active landfills and over 10,000 old municipal landfills in the US alone and thousands more all around the world. How long it takes something to decompose/degrade depends on a range of factors including climate and conditions. This is an estimate of time:

- Paper: 2 to 5 months
- Orange peel: 6 months
- Aluminum can: 200-500 years
- Plastic bottle: 1,000+years
- Glass bottle: 1 million+years
- Styrofoam: not biodegradable